SUSIE DENT'S

WEIRD WORDS

Illus

Andre

■SCHOLASTIC

Scholastic Children's Books
Euston House, 24 Eversholt Street
London NW1 1DB

A division of Scholastic Ltd
London ~ New York ~ Toronto ~ Sydney ~ Auckland
Mexico City ~ New Delhi ~ Hong Kong

Published in the UK by Scholastic Ltd, 2013

ISBN 978 1407 13702 5

Printed and bound by CPI Group (UK) Ltd, Croydon, CR0 4YY

2 4 6 8 10 9 7 5 3 1

Contents

A note to help you:

In this book the word 'root' means the origin of a word – where it sprang from, like the roots of a plant.

Introduction

I still remember the moment I became excited about **WORDS**. It was on the day I discovered that my favourite supper — a huge helping of lasagne with oodles of bubbling cheese — was actually named after a toilet. Of course I was completely horrified, but I knew I had to find out more.

Once I'd tracked the story all the way back to Roman times, and understood quite how a chamber pot came to mean the Italian dish we know today (you can read the story later in this book), I discovered another amazing thing — once you start digging into the words we use every day, you just can't stop. Just how did an **earwig** get its name? Why do some of us find the idea of kissing under the mistletoe completely YUCKY (it's not what you think!)? And why does the idea of a partridge in a pear tree make some of us snigger?

It turns out that English is packed with stories like these, adventures full of BLOOD, **POISON**, GHOULS and MONSTERS — even FARTS and PANTS. And the best part is that they are all under cover, hidden below the surface — it's up to us to go and find them. In fact I'd be thrilled* if, like me, you too become a **WORD DETECTIVE** and begin to explore the weird world of words yourself.

Though not in the usual sense of the word — just wait!

There are many, many more surprises out there waiting for you, and a lot of them are hiding between the pages of a dictionary.

Who knows: if you love the adventures as much as I do, maybe one day you too will sit in *Dictionary Corner*, spreading the word!

me

Yucky Words

Feeling Croaky?

It's a very weird thing to say, but if we lose our voice with a cold and sound a bit croaky, we sometimes describe it by saying, 'I have a frog in my throat.'

Where can such a **silly saying** come from?

Many centuries ago, medicine was a lot more basic than it is today, and some of the **'CURES'** people tried were VERY bizarre!

And so if, back in the Middle Ages, a person had a sore throat, the doctor would sometimes put a LIVE FROG head first into his patient's mouth! The idea was that the frog would spit out a substance that would then draw out the infection from the poor patient's mouth!

According to some, there was another superstition around at the time that drinking water sometimes contained frogspawn — that's frogs' eggs surrounded by transparent jelly — eurgh! People believed that frogs would grow inside the body, and make you hoarse or gag when they tried to jump out of your throat.

Either way, I may never use that expression again. In fact, I've turned the colour of a frog just thinking about it!

P.S. Poor frogs, they didn't have a very happy life in those days (see 'How to be a geek!', page 134, for another example).

Something on your mind?

Once upon a time, people believed that a certain insect could find its way into the **human brain** and live there quite happily.

Was it:

A. **A cockroach?**

B. **An earwig?**

C. **A spider?**

ANSWER: B. The earwig!

It was once widely believed that **earwigs** could creep into a sleeping person's ear, and then scuttle up to their brain where they would live and breed. This ancient belief explains how the insects got their name. The Anglo-Saxons, who spoke Old English over 800 years ago, called all insects 'wicgas', which sounded a bit like 'widgers' and which is related to the word 'wriggle'. When they discovered the earwig they called it 'ear-wicgas', or ear-insect.

There are lots of words for 'earwig' around the UK. In Yorkshire the earwig

is called a 'forkin robbin' (the 'fork'
part refers to their two pincers,
while 'robbin' was a popular nickname),
and in Cheshire they are known as
'twitchbells'.

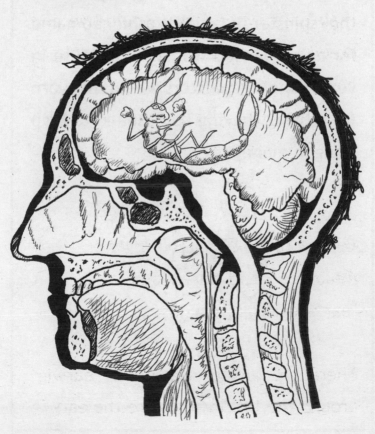

Did you know ...

... that the word '$spider$' comes from a very old English word meaning 'to spin' because a spider spins its webs. It was a '**spinner**', just like, in fact, the 'spinster' — an old-fashioned name for an unmarried woman — because in years gone by spinsters would spin yarn for a living, having no husband to help bring in money.

What's cooking?

There's nothing like eating a hot, steaming stew on a cold winter's day. Some of you may not like the idea of a stew — particularly a **school** one — and what I'm about to tell you probably won't change your mind!

That's because, believe it or not, the word 'stew' is connected to a **terrible** disease that causes fever and a rash, and that can be ...

... DEADLY!

That disease — called 'typhoid' or 'typhus' — is a horrible one that still occurs in some countries. Its name comes from a Greek word meaning 'steam', referring to the fever caused by the disease, as well as a horrible confusion of the **brain**. The idea is that steam is inside your head, stopping you from seeing clearly.

But where does 'stew' come in, you ask? Well, the Romans borrowed *typhus* from the Greek and turned it into their own word, *extufare*, which meant 'having a steam bath'! The word became 'stew' in English, and originally described a public bath or hot tub. Eventually a stew was used to describe **food** that had been steamed in hot liquid. If you think about it, the steam coming off a plate of hot stew is a little like the steam rising up from a very **hot** bath (full of water, not meat and vegetables!). But perhaps try not to wash yourself in one.

19

How are you feeling?

Do you have a good sense of humour? I think you must do if you're enjoying this book!

Now, picture the grumpiest, strictest, unfunniest person you know — it might be a relative, a teacher, a character in a book you've read. Well, although it's hard to believe, even they have humour. In fact, we all do.

Do you want to know why...?

20

Centuries ago, our bodily fluids were considered very important – so important in fact that they were thought to influence our every mood, such as grumpiness, happiness and sadness. And all those things sloshing around inside us were believed to keep us healthy, too. If your body had lots of 'black bile', for example (a horrible bitter substance), you would be sad. If it was yellow, you would be very irritable.

It all depended on the balance of these fluids – a bit like the ingredients in a cake. If the balance was more or

less right, you would have **calm** and **happy** days.

These fluids, which included blood, were known as the 'humours'. If you were 'out of humour', you would be **very** grumpy due to the lack of balance in your body. In 'good humour', however, meant that things were just right.

That's why, over time, 'humorous' came to describe something funny.

By the way, **sweets** and **fizzy** drinks don't count as bodily fluids, even if they do make you feel happy for a bit!

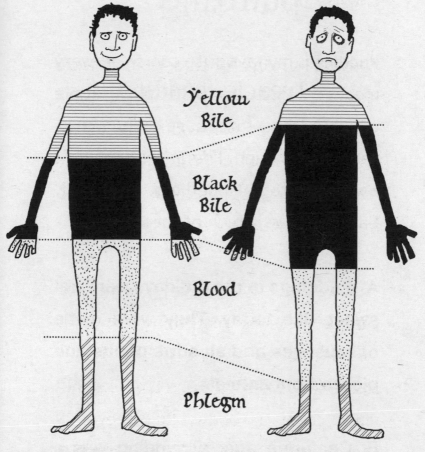

Yellow
Bile

Black
Bile

Blood

Phlegm

What's for pudding?

Pudding is my favourite course of every meal — treacle pudding, apple crumble, chocolate fudge cake... Mmm. Years ago, though, I *definitely* wouldn't have liked to eat puddings. Not at all. Can you guess which of these is true?

A. **Puddings in the old days were not sweet, like today. They were made of sausages and all sorts of bits and pieces from animals.**

B. **Centuries ago, a pudding was a term used for a buffoon – a joking** fool who would entertain crowds with his antics.

C. The first puddings were served up to Kings and Queens with birds cooked inside them.

ANSWER: A!

That's because the first puddings were made of sausage, fat, and even animal intestines. In fact, the Romans' word for 'intestines' — part of the human stomach — could also mean 'little sausage', and it passed into French as *boudin* and then into English as 'pudding'.

The earliest puddings were usually made by stuffing a sheep's stomach with parts of the same sheep, including its heart and lungs. Then the stomach was boiled! (I hope you're not reading this over lunch.)

As time and puddings went on, sweet ingredients replaced the sheepy ones (**hooray**!), and they were also often steamed in a bag. Today, we've kept the name, but don't always use the same method.

So, next time you're tucking into your hot **chocolate fudge cake**, spare a thought for medieval diners who were served with such delights as 'blood pudding', or tasty 'fish hog pudding' (made of, er, whale).

And by the way, songbirds really were once baked in pies, just like in the nursery rhyme. They used to be

served up on **special occasions**
and were considered *very* tasty!

Dog eat dog?

There are many expressions in English which feature dogs, and our poor canine friends don't tend to get a very good deal. We talk about 'a dog's life' (a hard one), being 'sick as a dog' (yeurgh!), a 'dog in the manger' attitude (a sulk), or 'it's raining cats and dogs' (really heavily). And, if you're always given the horrible jobs around the house, you might be described as a '**dogsbody**'.

It's a strange idea, because you don't _literally_ look like a dog. So where does the curious expression come from?

In centuries gone by, it wasn't just dogs who had a hard life. Sailors on the high seas did too, living in very cramped conditions and eating rather cheap and nasty **rations**! That's why, for example, when we want to have a long think or chat about something, we talk about 'chewing the fat', because in the old days, sailors would **literally** chew the fat of salt pork, sometimes for days on end! It was a bit like 19th-century chewing gum.

But back to 'dogsbody'. A staple of a sailor's diet was a mixture of **dried peas** and **eggs** boiled in a bag. Yuck. Sailors thought the jumbled food bulging in the bag looked — and tasted! — like a dog's body, and so the nickname stuck.

Over time, junior officers aboard a ship who had to do a lot of the most basic jobs were also called 'dogsbodies', because their tasks — such as scrubbing the deck or climbing up the mast in stormy weather — were often so unpleasant!

Anyone for haggis?

Hands up who's tried some Scottish haggis? Most of us, including me, would take one look and go '**YUCK**' or '**YECCH**'! (Two words that are in the dictionary by the way!) That's because haggis is traditionally made with the lungs, heart, and liver of a pig or sheep.

And if that's not bad enough, it's all wrapped up in a **sheep's stomach**!

Apparently it can be delicious though, so apologies to all haggis-lovers out there.

Now, have a guess where the word 'haggis' comes from.

A. **Was it originally described in a children's fairy tale, cooked up in a cauldron by a cackling old woman (the 'hag' part)?**

B. **Does it come from an old Viking word meaning 'to hack or cut to pieces', which is what the warriors used to do to their victims?**

C. **Does it go back to the Old French word *agace*, meaning a 'magpie'?**

ANSWER: B!

In **medieval** times, the verb 'hag' meant to roughly chop something — the word was brought over by **Viking** invaders and comes from their native Norse language. You can imagine them swinging their battle-axes around their heads as they forced their way into the villages of Britain, preparing to 'hag' whoever stood in their way. And that's where '**haggis**' comes in, because it's full of chopped meat.

Answer C isn't completely wrong by the way, because our cooked 'pies' really are named after the magpie, thanks to its habit of picking up random bits of material that it finds — just as a pie is full of odds and ends of meat, vegetables, or other ingredients.

Acne

Having a spotty face from time to time is **nothing new**. Even the ancient Greeks got acne! And when they needed a word to describe the red pimples sticking out from their faces they thought of their existing word *akme*, which meant 'a point'.

Now, we all make spelling mistakes sometimes, and as it turns out that's nothing new either! Centuries ago, a scribe writing a book misspelled *akme* as *akne* and the change stuck.

As it happens, the name for an outbreak of pimples is linked to an awful lot of other English words that you would never guess!

Not only is acne related to acme, a word that still exists and means 'the highest point' of something, but it has connections with lots of other words, too. These include <u>ac</u>id, which gets its name because of its sharpness or pointedness, and <u>ac</u>ute, which comes from a word meaning a needle. An <u>ac</u>acia is a very thorny tree, and an <u>ac</u>robat walks right at the very tip or top of something — the first acrobats were tightrope walkers. An <u>ac</u>ropolis

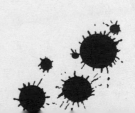

is a city at the top of a hill, while an <u>ac</u>ronym takes the first letter or 'tip' of a word to make a new one.

Next time you use a text <u>ac</u>ronym, like 'paw' (parents are watching!), or hear about a 'BOGOF' in a supermarket (buy one, get one free), you are actually looking back to a spotty-faced teenager from ancient times!

A Sticky Ending!

Treacle pudding is one of my all-time favourite foods, especially on a cold winter's day. Mind you, I did go off it a bit after I discovered where treacle, that thick, sticky, sweet liquid, actually came from. Can you guess which of these stories is the real one?

A. **Treacle was originally the sticky, yellow goo left behind by a giant snail from Roman times.**

B. **For hundreds of years, treacle meant 'medicine', usually one with an extremely yucky taste!**

C. Treacle comes from a very old Arabic word meaning a 'weird-tasting drink'.

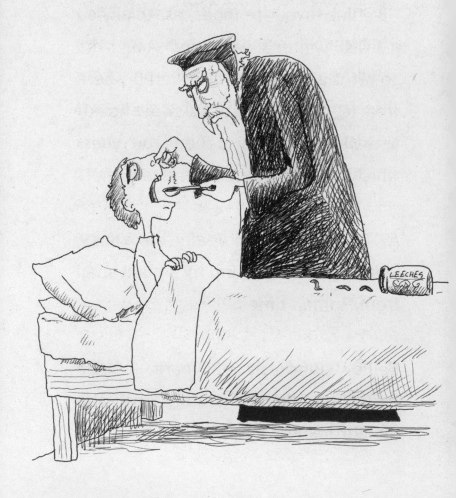

ANSWER: B!

The earliest form of the word 'treacle' meant 'a poisonous animal'. That animal might be a snake, or even a wild lion. The victim of a poisonous bite from one of these deadly beasts needed medicine as an antidote very quickly. Over time 'treacle' began to mean the antidote itself — medicine so horrible-tasting that it needed a teaspoon of sugar to help it go down — just like Jane and Michael in *Mary Poppins*! Eventually 'treacle' came to mean the sugar instead of the medicine. And that's how it came to top my favourite pudding list!

Did you know...

If you were tempted by answer C, it wasn't the word 'treacle', but 'syrup', which came over from Arabic more than 400 years ago. And it actually tasted very nice — a bit like sherbet, in fact, which comes from the same root as syrup! All very sweet.

Wet and Windy Words

That little squirt!

Do you like to squirt ketchup on your chips?

Next time you are about to do just that, you may want to forget what you are about to read...

The very first sense of the word 'squirt', way back in the 1400s, was '**diarrhoea**'. To 'squirt', meanwhile, was used of gushing water but also meant to 'let loose diarrhoea' — ejecting it quite forcefully, in fact.

None of which you really wanted to know, did you? You may never think of a water-squirter in quite the same way again.

By the way, the opposite of having the 'squits' (a shortening of 'squirts', in case you wanted to know), is to be constipated. You may have come across the word 'soluble' in your science lessons, when it means 'dissolvable'. It hasn't always meant quite that, though — it once described bowels that were 'relaxed' and free of constipation.

Er, let's leave it there, shall we?

KiSSes are Sweet (or are they...?)

Have you ever seen your parents **kissing** under the mistletoe? Yuck! Next time you do, you can tell them *exactly* where the word 'mistletoe' comes from — it may change their minds altogether!

The second part of 'mistletoe' meant a 'twig'. So far so good. It's the '**mistle**' bit that is VERY yucky. It goes back to an ancient word that meant 'wee' or 'poo'. That's because mistletoe tended to grow where birds did their bottom business. Just as manure from horses and farm animals helps crops to grow, so the mistletoe would flourish among the bird droppings. In fact, people long ago believed that the mistletoe grew out of the **poo** itself, not just nearby!

Charming. I'm not going *near* any mistletoe sprigs this Christmas!

Partridge Surprise!

Do you remember that line from a traditional Christmas song, '... **and a partridge in a pear tree...**'? Does it make you feel all festive and wish for snow?

Well, next time you sing it, TRY not to laugh out loud, because you're about to learn the **hilarious** history of the partridge's name...

There is a verb in French, *péter*, which makes all schoolchildren across the Channel giggle and titter like mad. It means 'to break wind' — in other words, to '**trump**', 'do a windipop', '**pop**' or, all right, '**fart**'.

The ancient Greeks must have been a bit windy, too, because both *péter* and 'partridge' go back to their word for farting. We think it's because the whirring sound of the birds' wings reminded the Romans of what some people like to call '**trouser burps**'.

(I vividly remember that, in my school dictionary, a 'fart' was defined as 'a minor explosion between the legs'. I think dictionaries have moved on a bit since then — go and check yours to see for yourself!)

Did you know ...

... that the word fart is over 700 years old? It was probably meant to represent the sound made by windy medieval folks! Can you make up your own words that sound to you, er, like a fart?

A potty idea for supper!

Bubbling, cheesy lasagne, straight from the oven, mmmmm. I wonder whether you like this Italian dish as much as I do!

If you do, and next time you have it for dinner, spare a thought for the Romans — they used the word lasagne to mean something VERY different!

(Warning: if you don't want to insult the cook, don't read on...!)

There's no polite way of saying this, so I'll just come straight out and say it. In the days of the Romans, a *lasanum* was a chamber pot, or portable **loo**. Strange as it may seem, the Italians took that word and applied it to their cooking pots! Perhaps one day an Italian diner decided to make a mean joke about the dish they'd been served and suggested the cooking tasted a bit like the contents of a toilet? How rude!

Over time, the name for the cooking dish that was traditionally used to cook a meal of pasta, meat, and cheese became attached to the meal itself, and that's how we still use 'lasagne' today.

By the way, until a law was passed in the 1800s to ban it, chamber pots were regularly emptied out of windows, splattering innocent pedestrians with their contents. Ugh! If I'd lived back then I would have definitely preferred a mountain of **lasagne** on my head...

It's all pants!

Big pants, tight pants, spotty pants, silly pants... They come in all shapes and sizes.

But have a guess where the word 'pants' comes from?

A. **Pants were once so baggy that they made a short 'whooshing' sound every time the wearer took a step. It reminded people of the sound a dog makes when it's hot and 'panting'.**

B. **400 years ago, on the stage of Italian theatres, one of the best-loved** characters was a strange, skinny old man who wore very tight-fitting trousers and tights! His name was Pantalone, and today's pants were named after him.

C. **Nicholas Pantomime** was the name of the man who invented the very funny Christmas show, full of men dressed as women in hugely baggy bloomers!

ANSWER: B!

Traditional Italian comedies featured lots of funny characters. Pantalone, with his skinny legs and very tight trousers, made everyone roar with laughter.

He was so popular that his name travelled far and wide, and the English borrowed it to describe the kind of tight trousers or 'pantaloons' that he wore.

Today's 'pants' are a shorter version (in every sense!) of the original 'pantaloons'. In America, of course, they still use 'pants' to mean trousers.

There never really was a Nicholas Pantomime, by the way. The word 'pantomime' comes from two Greek words meaning 'all' (*pan*) and 'miming' (*mimos*). In ancient times, an actor would mime ALL the parts!

And if today you hear someone say 'that's pants', it's slang for '**that's rubbish**'. We're not sure why — perhaps it's because most of us find underpants a bit *smelly*!

Weird Words

Whoops, wrong spell!

The amazing ventriloquist!

Imagine you are a citizen of ancient Greece. You come across a man in the street with the most amazing ability to speak without moving his lips at all. Do you:

A. **Go up and give him a dram (the ancient Greek coin) for his efforts?**

B. **Run away screaming, telling people that an evil spirit is on the loose?**

C. **Ask him if he knows any magic tricks besides ventriloquism?**

ANSWER: B!

In those days in ancient Greece, someone who was taken over by an evil spirit was thought to speak not from their mouth, but from their **stomach**. They were called *engastrimuthos* — *gaster* meaning stomach, and *muthos* meaning speech — in other words, they were 'belly speakers', and were to be avoided at all costs!

When the Romans took the word over, they translated the idea into Latin with the word *ventriloquus*, which also meant 'speaking from the stomach'. Of course, by the time English took it over as '𝔳𝔢𝔫𝔱𝔯𝔦𝔩𝔬𝔮𝔲𝔦𝔰𝔪', all ideas of evil spirits had disappeared, and it famously became a clever trick. Go on, can you speak from *your* stomach?!

Did you know...

The magical word 'abracadabra' also started as a very serious word. It was based on the name of a god worshipped in ancient Egypt and was thought to have such magical powers that people would write it on a lucky charm (or amulet) and wear it around their necks. It was written like this

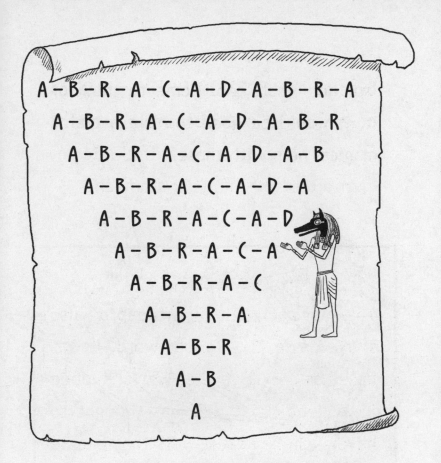

A-B-R-A-C-A-D-A-B-R-A
A-B-R-A-C-A-D-A-B-R
A-B-R-A-C-A-D-A-B
A-B-R-A-C-A-D-A
A-B-R-A-C-A-D
A-B-R-A-C-A
A-B-R-A-C
A-B-R-A
A-B-R
A-B
A

Meanwhile, we get 'hey presto!' from Italian, where *presto* means 'quickly', and a magic 'spell' comes from a very old English word meaning 'to tell' or 'recite' — that's the root of our

'spelling' tests too! Come to think of
it, it would be good to have a bit of
magical help with those.

That's odd (and a little bit rude...)!

Can you guess the odd one out in the following list?

- Copper
- Iron
- Silver
- Cobalt
- Platinum
- Pumpernickel
- Zinc

ANSWER: pumpernickel!

There is a metal called nickel, but pumpernickel is a dense, dark kind of bread from Germany — it's delicious, but takes a while to chew!

The word 'pumpernickel' is actually related to the metal nickel though, and its story might make you laugh. It all goes back to the name 'Nicholas', which has had many associations in English, including of course Santa Claus, who is also known as Saint Nicholas. Another use of the name, though, was for the devil, who had the *nick*name (sorry!) Old Nick — there is a similar word in German, too. And it's this devilish word that's behind the name 'nickel', because many years ago, whenever miners were searching for 'copper', they'd end up finding another metal that they *didn't* want because it wasn't worth anything. And so they called this metal, in German, the *kupfernickel* or 'copper demon', because it was always getting in their way, as though the Devil was playing tricks on them. Over time they simply shortened the word to *nickel*.

Now you must be wondering where the pumpernickel bread comes into this? Well, the bread is very hard to digest, and it will probably make you quite windy when you eat it. Others thought so too — *pumpern* means to break wind in German, and so 'pumpernickel' really means '**farting demon**'! Tell that to your parents if they ever offer you some.

Muscle madness!

Going to the gym is a good thing, right? Today's gyms are full of machines that make our bodies healthier and our muscles stronger.

Gym is short for 'gymnasium', a word that is also related to 'gymnastics'. But I bet you can't guess what the word meant originally, back in the days of ancient Greece?

WARNING:

reading this may make you snort with laughter!

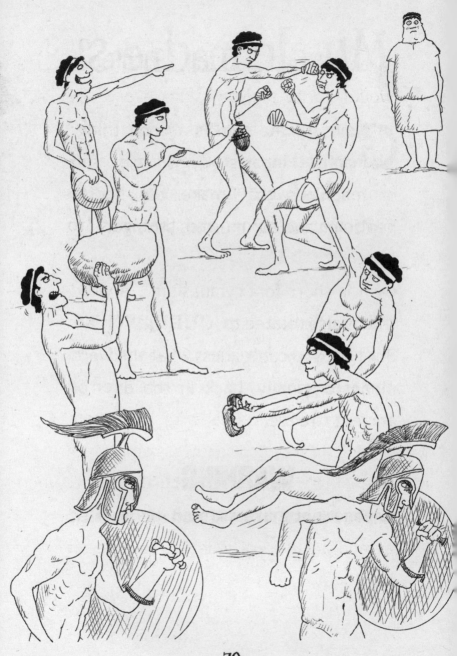

In ancient times, Greek athletes would go to a gymnasium every day in order to exercise and develop their bodies. Nothing new there, but there's more: the word 'gymnasium' had a particular meaning, and that was 'to exercise **naked**'!

Naked? Well, an appreciation of the human body was very important in those days, and athletes were keen to perfect their muscles and show them off a little too. And so it was completely normal to work out in the buff!* In fact, anyone *not* naked would be scoffed at and accused of wanting to hide an ugly body.

*The word '**BUFF**' comes from the colour of bare buffalo skin...

...Right then. Anyone for a bit of exercise?

How big a fan are you?

Are you a **football fan?** Or a fan of the Queen? Maybe you're a *Countdown* fan (hooray!). We're all fans of something — in my case it's word-games and chocolate cake.

But have you ever wondered where the word '**fan**' comes from?

Could it be:

A. **That the original fans used to follow the object of their admiration everywhere, and literally fan them** with enormous palm leaves to keep them cool in hot weather.

B. 'Fan' is short for 'fanatic', and once described people who were thought to be posses sed by a demon, and who behaved in a crazy fashion.

C. 'Fan' is a shortening of 'fantastic', because, after all, every team or celebrity loves to have supporters.

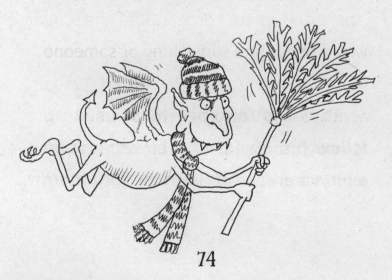

ANSWER: B!

The Latin word *fanaticus* came from *fanum*, '**a temple**', and meant 'inspired by a god'. The god in question though was thought to be an evil spirit, and so a 'fanatic' was a religious 'maniac', possessed by a demon, which made them behave in crazy ways!

Over time, *fanaticus* was shortened to 'fan', and came to describe someone who worshipped something or someone with great passion. We've forgotten about the **evil spirits** these days, although some football fans do behave a bit crazily sometimes don't they?!

By the way, those servants who would fan their masters were called, in India, *punkah wallahs* — *punkah* means 'fan', and *wallah* means a 'man' or 'servant'.

And as for 'fantastic', that is linked to 'fantasy' and something that is as wonderful as you could ever imagine.

It's hairy stuff!

Have you ever noticed what happens to your arms when you get cold or frightened? You might get 'goosebumps', pimply skin, which got its name from its resemblance to the skin of a plucked goose (eurgh). But something else happens too. The little hairs on your arms stand up on end! The same thing happens to cats and dogs too, just like those cartoon cats whose fur sticks straight up. They look pretty horrible....

In Latin, the language of the Romans, the verb *horrere* described hair that

stuck out. The Romans noticed that that's exactly what happened to their own body hair whenever they were frightened. And so *horrere* became linked to the idea of shivering with terror at the sight of something awful.

That's why, whenever we talk about things being '**horrible**' or '**horrifying**' today, or whenever we watch a '**horror**' movie, we have to thank the Romans — and take a look at what the hairs on our arms are doing!

Did you know ...

... that there are other words in English which come from the way our bodies change in certain situations. 'Appalling', meaning something that's awful. It comes from a word that means 'to grow pale' in terror. And 'petrified' comes from the idea of something being changed into stone. That's because, when we're that scared, we stand still like a statue!

Are you ready for this?

We all know that boys and girls are different, but it's not true that ALL girls like **pink** and all boys like **football**. None of us think like that any more, right...?!

Well, when it comes to the stories behind the words 'girl' and 'boy', expectations of the way they behaved and lived were very fixed.

800 years ago, the world for both sexes was very different than it is today...
In the 1300s, the word 'girl' meant

simply a 'child', male or female, and it stayed that way for many centuries until people began to apply the word *only* to female children. One suggestion is that 'girl' is linked to another English word 'garrulous', an adjective that today still means '**talkative**'. In other words, girls were seen as chatterboxes!

Girl   Girl

What about boys then? Their lives, back in medieval days, could be very miserable. Those from poor families were often held captive and worked as **slaves** for the wealthy. It's possible that 'boy' comes from an Old French word that meant 'to tie someone up by the feet with straps', perhaps because boy servants were cruelly tied up when they weren't working. Eventually the term lost that meaning when boys — thankfully — had a much freer life, and so 'boy' simply described a male child, as it does today.

How things have changed — boys aren't usually slaves any more, and girls *definitely* aren't the *only* ones who talk a lot these days!

Girl   Boy

Help!

How are you with **spiders**? The huge, hairy ones? I quite like the small kind, actually, but if I spotted a tarantula scuttling towards me I'd be the first out the door!

Back in the 1400s, the people of Taranto in Southern Italy did more than that. In fact, they behaved very strangely indeed...

In the 15th century, the city of Taranto suffered a strange outbreak of a disease that affected the nerves of its victims, and made them behave *very* weirdly.

They would dance around in a **crazy** and completely uncontrollable way — a bit like your parents at a party, only much, much worse!

The local people thought that this **bizarre** behaviour was caused by the bite of the tarantula, for those spiders were hugely common there. They believed that the only way to get rid of the poison was to whirl around and dance, dance, dance! In fact, that's why one particularly lively Italian dance is still known as the 'tarantella' today.

Did you know ...

... that 'tarantula' is an example of a 'toponym' — a word named after a place. English has a lot of them — take a look at these:

TANGERINE — the fruit is named after Tangiers in Morocco where they were first grown.

DENIM — this fabric was first made in Nîmes in France: *de Nîmes* means 'from Nîmes'.

JODPHURS — these riding trousers originated in the town of Jodphur in India.

CANARY — these birds were named after the Canary Islands where they lived and bred. (Just so you know, the islands themselves were named by the Romans after the big dogs that lived there: *canis* was Latin for dog. But that's another story...)

HOw catchy!

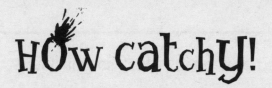

You might not realize it, but you're surrounded by **slogans** every day. These are the short and striking phrases used as adverts for a company or product — you might recognize some of these here:

> *'Just do it'*
> *'I'm Loving It'*
> *'Taste the Rainbow'*

Now, close your eyes, and picture this scene in your mind. You're a warrior in the Scottish Highlands, preparing for a mighty battle with a rival clan.

You're wearing a deerskin waistcoat and holding a fearsome weapon called a broadsword in your hand. The air is filled with the unique battle cry of your clan — you pound your chest and join in with the chant.

What's all that got to do with ads for trainers? Good question. But read on...

Before the word '**slogan**', came its longer form, '**slughorn**'. And no, that wasn't not an instrument played by slimy garden creatures, but a Scottish battle-cry shouted by warriors before they lifted their weapons and charged.

Each clan had their own slughorn, but they all had one thing in common — the sound, as it rang out from the mountains and hillsides, was quite terrifying. (Particularly when it was accompanied by bagpipes!)

Over time, as the highland battles ended and faded from people's memories, '**slughorn**' was shortened to '**slogan**' and it became simply a phrase associated with a particular person or group, particularly in advertising.

I don't know about you, but I think that hollering the slughorn of a Scottish warrior might be a good way of starting your next school Sports Day!

Hairy scary!

Imagine you are an **adventurer** on the high seas. It's the 5th century BC, and you are sailing past the west coast of Africa, keeping a watch for any sign of life — especially of the unfriendly kind!

Now read this account from a real-life adventurer of that time, called Hanno:

'Leaving this place, we sailed along the burning coast for three days and came to the gulf named the Horn of the South. At the end of it was an island full of savages. The greater parts of these were women. They had hairy bodies and their interpreters called them ...'

Can you guess which word came next?

A. **Cannibals**

B. **Gorillas**

C. **Chimpanzees**

ANSWER: B!

The diary account of Hanno, that Greek explorer, has a rather gruesome ending:

'We pursued some of the males, but we could not catch a single one because they were good climbers and they defended themselves fiercely. However, we managed to take three women. We killed them and removed their skins to take back to Carthage.'

Many centuries later, an American naturalist discovered the bones and skull of a great ape. Remembering Hanno's story, he named the species

Troglodytes Gorilla. Who would have thought that 'gorillas' were once thought to be extremely hairy women?

Did you know ...

... that the word 'cannibal' comes from the Spanish *Canibales*, and was the name given to the original inhabitants of the Caribbean islands. The modern meaning of the word came about because the Spanish believed the islanders ate whoever they came across!

Ooh, that's sinister!

Who has the most *sinister* face you can think of? Dracula? Voldemort? Count Olaf from Lemony Snicket's books? Whenever I think of the word '**sinister**' I have scary music playing in my head and imagine a dark shadowy figure creeping up behind me to give me a shock! The story of where it comes from is very unexpected, too.

I'll give you a clue.

In *Harry Potter and the Goblet of Fire*, the fourth Harry Potter story, did you notice that the villainous Voldemort

uses his left hand to cast spells
in the graveyard?

Da-da-daaaaaaaaa!

(That's the scary music part.)

Back in Roman times, people believed strongly that the left side of the body was unlucky. The word for 'left' in their language, Latin, was, in fact, *sinistra*. So the fact that Voldemort wields his wand in his left hand is very appropriate!

By the way, have you ever heard of the expression 'get off on the wrong foot'? It means to start something in a bad or awkward way. Well, that foot was the left one, just as when we say a grumpy person 'got out of bed on the wrong side', we mean the left one too!

In fact, left-handers have had such a bad time over the centuries that many words in English that still mean ‘awkward’ or ‘foolish’, such as ‘cack-handed’, actually began as terms for poor left-handed folks.

In fact, within a 14-mile radius in Scotland there are 14 different variations for being left-handed, and — this is even more extraordinary — almost all have to do with the Kerr family from Ferniehirst Castle in the Scottish Borders. Among them are ‘Corrie-fisted’ and ‘Kerr-handed’; let me explain.

The story goes that the Laird of the Castle, Andrew Kerr, was left-

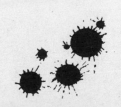

handed. He used that fact to great advantage, surprising the enemy with the unexpected direction of his sword. In fact, he only employed left-handed soldiers. The castle itself was built for left-handers — in most castles the spiral staircases go round clockwise, but Ferniehirst has *anti*-clockwise ones. That gave left-handed swordsmen a huge advantage, because the bends gave their left arms freedom to move over the open railing and swing round with maximum force.

Isn't that the **perfect revenge** for all those left-handed insults?!

Spooky, Scary Words

How egg-ghoulish!

There's nothing quite like a dark cold **Halloween** night, when pumpkins glow and ghosts and ghouls go trick or treating! But do you know where the word *ghoul* comes from? See if you can guess the correct one:

A. Is it a shorter version of the word 'cagoule', a waterproof jacket, because ghouls were believed to have greater evil powers when it rained?

B. Is it a blend of 'ghost' and 'fool', because ghouls were once associated with April Fool's Day?

C. Does it come from a foreign word meaning 'a demon that eats dead bodies'?

ANSWER: C!

The word 'ghoul' comes from an Arabic word for an evil spirit, which devoured the dead flesh of corpses buried in graveyards at night-time.

Centuries later, the word was also applied to graverobbers who would dig up buried corpses and sell them to doctors and surgeons for practising on!

Did you know ...

... that there are hundreds of words in English for supernatural creatures. **'Fairy'** comes from an old Latin term for the three 'Fates', powerful

---

goddesses who were thought to control the destiny of every human being.

'**Goblin**' comes from a word given by German miners in medieval times to the mischievous spirits that haunted the silver mines.

A '**werewolf**' comes from the earliest days of English — its literal meaning is 'man-wolf'.

And zombies weren't always frightening: the word comes from a West African word that means 'good-luck charm'!

CocOnut

While we're on the subject of food and those ghouls chomping on dead flesh, how about some coconut? Now the story behind this one is *weird*.

Take a look at this **coconut shell** — what do you see?

You can't really miss those three holes, like two eyes and a small mouth, staring back at you! Almost like Halloween pumpkins. And that's exactly what the Portuguese explorers thought when they discovered the coconut — their name for it, coco, meant '**grinning skull**', as well as '𝔟𝔬𝔤𝔢𝔶𝔪𝔞𝔫'. It was even used to frighten children, who were told that if they were naughty, the 'coco' would come.

Take a look at that coconut again — it's a scary thought!

Did you know ...

... that the names of many other foods have funny stories behind them? Take a look at these

Food	What it means literally
Vermicelli:	little worms.
Linguine:	little tongues.
Lobster:	a locust, apparently thought to be similar in shape.
Burrito:	a small donkey, perhaps because it is rolled up like the bedrolls and packs that donkeys carry.
Baguette:	a stick carried in the hand, sometimes used as a weapon
Tapioca:	to squeeze out the dregs!

And as we know, a lasagne was once a toilet... (See page 51.)

Give me a clue!

I don't know about you, but I love mazes. I always end up completely lost, but then that's half the fun! I'm also always amazed when I finally emerge. And that's quite appropriate really, because a maze took its name from the fact that it 'amazes'.

Now, have a guess where the word 'clue' comes from.

A. Was it a secret message written in invisible ink by prisoners on the walls of their cells?

B. Was it a clever way of helping the hero of a famous story escape from a deadly maze?

C. Could it have been an early form of the game 'charades' – but when someone couldn't guess the clue or 'mime', they had to pay a horrible forfeit?

Tell you what, I'll give you a string of clues to take with you. (That's it, that's the clue!)

The story of the word 'clue' began a long, long time ago...

...In Greek legend, King Minos of Crete ordered his craftsmen to build him a maze in which he could keep his pet Minotaur. Actually, I say 'pet', but 'monster' would be a much better description — this beast was half-man, half-bull!

Now, King Minos's armies would regularly attack Athens across the sea. The King of Athens begged Minos to stop; Minos agreed, but on one condition: that Athens would promise to hand over seven boys and seven girls every nine years as food for the Minotaur.

Reluctantly, the King of Athens agreed, and when nine years had passed, it was time for the children to be picked. The brave warrior Theseus promised to be one of them — for he had a cunning plan. As he made his way deeper and deeper into the maze, he unwound a long ball of thread. He eventually found the Minotaur and slayed it in a bloody battle. Best of all, he managed to find his way out of the maze by following his trail of thread.

And that is how the mystery is solved, for the ball of string was called a '**clew**' or '**clue**'.

See, I told you I'd given you a hint!

Did you know...

That the Minotaur's maze was called the Labyrinth, pronounced lab-ee-rinth, and to this day we use that word to describe a complicated building with lots of different corridors or passage. They don't *usually* have monsters lurking in them though.

There be dragons!

We all love a story about huge, winged monsters that breathe fire and can pretty much cook anything in their path. But most of us are glad that dragons only exist in stories!

For the Greeks, though, dragons were very real. Take a guess as to which creature they called a *drakon*:

A. **A slithering hissing serpent**

B. **A giant sea-monster**

C. **A dragonfly**

ANSWER: A!

In ancient Greece, a *drakon* was a snake, or indeed any creature that seemed to look at them in a deadly way and make them shiver and shudder in fright. In English, the word became 'dragon', and in our minds the creature became much bigger too, with wings and the ability to breathe fire. A little imagination goes a long way!

That huge sea-monster in answer B, by the way, was called a 'drake' — have you ever heard of the game 'drakes and dragons'? That's where it comes from.

Oh, and **dragonflies** got their name because of their long body, powerful wings, and bulging eyes. Ooh-er!

Grotty grottoes!

Do you ever use the word 'grotesque' when you see something **gross**?

And have you ever visited Santa's grotto at Christmas time?

Two very different questions, you might think, but in fact they're linked by a curious fact. So read on...

The word 'grotto' comes from Italy, and once meant a picturesque, nice-looking cave — the sort of place you might choose to have a picnic in.

The grottoes of ancient Rome, however, were deep, dark vaults beneath their buildings. When they were discovered by archaeologists, their walls were found to be covered with strange scenes of animal and human faces wearing terrifying, distorted expressions. This strange art was called *pittura grottesca* by the Italians — which meant 'grotto art'. But the memory of those horrible faces stuck with them, and that's why *grottesca*, or 'grotesque', came to mean something terrifying, disgusting, or — quite simply — WEIRD!

Oh, and the word 'grotty' comes from 'grotesque', too.

Did you know ...

... that 'graffiti' is also Italian. It means 'scratch' or 'scribbling', and that too looks back to early pictures — this time scratched on to ancient walls in Pompeii and Rome.

It turns out that today's graffiti artists have very cool ancestors!

What a  nightmare!

We all have them — those scary bad dreams, which stay in our minds for quite a while. Sometimes we even say 'I'm having a nightmare' if everything seems to be going wrong! But where does the word '**nightmare**' come from?

A. **A nightmare was originally a wild black horse, believed to gallop through the night and bring bad dreams to all the sleeping people it passed.**

B. **The first nightmares were believed to be monsters that came out of the sea at nighttime and gobbled up the locals.**

C. **Over a thousand years ago, a 'mare' was a female evil goblin – according to legend she would lie on the chest of someone sleeping and give them terrible dreams and the feeling of being suffocated.**

ANSWER. C!

Well all of the possible answers were pretty scary, but the real answer is probably the most terrifying of all. A mare was once thought to be a wicked female spirit who came out at night to lie on top of her sleeping victim until they could hardly breathe, filling their dreams with horrible images of death. The legend was so frightening that the **Anglo-Saxons** tried all sorts of rituals to scare the nightmares away. One of them involved tying up a knife in a cloth and swinging it three times around the body while saying a spell (don't try that at home!), and sometimes they would hang mistletoe over their bed.

Of course, over the centuries people forgot about the goblins and applied 'nightmare' to the feelings of terror and suffocation instead. My remedy for a bad dream has to be the best — a chocolate biscuit!

Tyrannosaurus terror!

T-Rex, the most **terrifying** dinosaur of them all, lived over 60 million years ago, but was only discovered in the early years of the 20th century. If you close your eyes you can picture this beast with a massive head and giant tail, weighing over 6 tons and with teeth over 23-centimetres long. Forget vampires, Frankenstein and King Kong — for me, T-Rex is the **ultimate monster**!

All of this explains why scientists chose the name they did when they discovered the fossils of an unknown dinosaur in the appropriately named Hell Creek in the USA. Can you guess the right answer from the following 'T-Rex' tales?

A. **The literal translation of the Latin is 'King of the Roars', because T-Rex was a dinosaur that could roar more loudly than any other living being on the planet.**

B. **T-Rex was named after Monsieur Tyrrano, who first discovered the huge dinosaur fossil.**

C. **The name is Greek for 'Tyrant Lizard, the King'.**

ANSWER: C!

A '**tyrant**' is a wicked bully, perfect for a dinosaur that trampled over, or ate, anything in its way.

The word '**dinosaur**' itself means '**terrible lizard**', and it has been used as the model for naming almost every dinosaur whose remains have been discovered since then. Here are a few more dinosaur names decoded:

BRONTOSAURUS means 'thunder lizard'.

BRACHIOSAURUS means 'arm lizard', because its arms were longer than its legs.

STEGOSAURUS means 'roof lizard' because it had bony plates along its back.

IGUANODON means 'iguana tooth', because this dinosaur's teeth looked like those of an iguana lizard.

PTERODACTYL means 'winged finger' because the creature's wing was supported by a GIANT finger!

Don't go crazy!

Have you ever seen someone 'go **berserk**'? If you've seen someone behave in a *completely* crazy way, then you probably have.

Picture the scene... A ship that has travelled miles across the oceans pulls up at night on the English shores. On its deck stand terrifyingly fierce Viking warriors preparing to fight to the death anyone who dares to stand in their way. They wear helmets and carry shields, axes and spears. Wrapped around their bodies are thick bearskins, which keep them warm and make them look even more ferocious.

It's the stuff of nightmares, don't you think? Well, between the years 800 and 1100, such scenes were very real. And they are the reason behind the word 'berserk'.

Berserkr, in the Viking's native language, meant 'bear-shirt'. Historians believe that the Viking warriors, before battle, would put on their bearskins and perform a terrifying, crazy-looking war dance known as the '**berserker rage**'. Perhaps they believed that the strength of the bear would be passed onto them, allowing them to fight as ferociously as a wild animal, and to conquer any enemy.

I don't know about you, but I'm not planning on putting on a '**bear-shirt**' anytime soon. Although hang on — perhaps it could come in useful in Dictionary Corner each time I have to reject a contestant's word!

Grisly and Gory Words

How to be a geek!

Do you know any computer 'geeks'? Or perhaps you're a geek yourself — someone who is so enthusiastic and knowledgeable about a particular subject that it means more to you than almost anything.

Today, a geek is usually a **positive word**, used with pride, but that wasn't always the case. At one time, it meant a stupid or worthless person. And once you read the word's true story, you may never look at a geek in the same way again.
So read on...

Many, many years ago, a geek or 'geck' was a performer at a circus sideshow — these were sometimes called 'freak shows' as they would include people with a **scary** or strange appearance. Part of the geek's act was to bite off the head of a live chicken as, er, entertainment for the crowds.

Clearly that was an extremely stupid thing to do, as well as a yucky one, and so 'geek' went on to mean a fool or a simpleton.

Today's sense of the word only appeared very recently, when computers became COOL!

But be warned, no matter how much you like being geeky, leave those poor chickens alone!

GEEK SHOW

Thumbs Up!

At the **gladiatorial** contests of ancient Rome, what did the Emperor mean when he gave the losing gladiator the **thumbs up**?

A. **He was letting them go free.**

B. **He was condemning them to death.**

C. **He was allowing the crowd to decide on life or death.**

ANSWER: B!

Today, when we give someone the 'thumbs up' we are showing that we approve, or that something is going well. It would be easy to think that, when Roman emperors once did the same, they were sparing the losing gladiator's life. In fact, the thumbs-up sign in those ancient amphitheatres meant that the gladiator was condemned to die. The verdict was usually greeted with roars of approval from a **bloodthirsty** audience eager for the spectacle of death.

The lives and battles of gladiators gave us other words in English too, although we may not realize it now. Take 'arena', which comes from a Latin word whose literal meaning was 'sand'. That's because the middle of the vast amphitheatres, where the fierce combat took place between gladiators (and sometimes wild animals kept in cages underground), was covered with sand in order to soak up the blood spilled during the fight. In later centuries, sand and straw were both used to mop up the gore that followed a beheading!

Today's sporting champions have gladiators and other Roman athletes as their ancestors. The word 'champion'

goes back to the Latin *campus*, which meant a field, especially one used for training for battle. The very first 'campus' was in the city of Rome, and was near the Tiber River. Over time, this large plain became ancient Rome's field and track playground, used by Julius Caesar himself together with young men from all over Rome.

'Gladiator', by the way, comes from the Latin for 'sword'. And if your parents ever talk about a plant called a '**gladioli**', you can tell them it takes its name from its sword-shaped leaves!

Did you know ...

... that a 'campus' university is one whose buildings are all in the same grounds, often with wide-open spaces. They too look back to ancient Roman sports grounds and training fields.

'What a Shambles!'

This is the sort of expression you might hear your parents or grandparents say when they walk into your bedroom!

A shambles is a right mess, but it used to mean something far more grisly and yucky. Have a guess at its origin!

Was a shambles:

A. **A meat market full of blood and gore from slaughtered animals?**

B. **An area of ground where a**

particularly bloody battle has taken place?

C. An old ruin of a house believed to be haunted by an evil spirit?

ANSWER: A!

There is a street in the city of York which is called 'The Shambles'. It was once the site of a row of butchers' shops. It all goes back to a time when a 'shamble' was a wooden table on which fresh, bloody, meat was put out for sale.

Over time, a shambles came to mean a place where animals are slaughtered — a messy, bloody, horrible business — or the result of a fierce and violent battle (and so you weren't completely wrong if you answered B!). And that's why today, when we want to describe chaos, mess, or confusion, we look

back to the time when a shambles was a scene of terrible killing.

Next time you're forced to **tidy your room**, you can at least be happy it's not covered in sticky blood and goo!

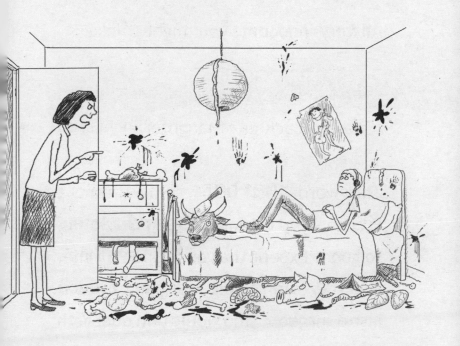

Time for a trim

Have you ever seen a traditional barber's shop? It's a place where men go for haircuts, and will often have a red and white stripy pole outside.

All very innocent, you might think...

(Cue evil cackles of laughter...)

The word 'barber' comes from a French word meaning 'beard'. So far, so good. Except that once upon a time, a barber didn't just cut hair: he was also a surgeon, who would pull out teeth and stitch up wounds. Worst of all, he would also perform 'blood-letting': a very old practice that involved slicing open a vein with a knife and letting it bleed. Why, you ask? (Are you feeling queasy yet?) The answer is that it was believed in those days that too much blood was bad for the body.

The red of a barber's pole is a symbol of the blood that used to stain the floor of the barbers' shops, and the white represents the bandages used to dress the wounds. Boys, you may want to think twice about your choice of hairdresser next time!

Did you know…

You might think that the barbers were 'barbaric', a word that means cruel and violent. In fact that word isn't related — for ancient Greeks it meant 'foreign', because their vicious enemies came from abroad. And that's also why they called a red, long, and strange-looking fruit 'rhubarb', because it looked so 'foreign' and exotic.

Grenade alert!

Have you ever seen one of those cartoons where the **baddie** is holding a round, black, smoldering cannonball and letting out a wicked laugh? The very first hand grenades looked a little like those cannonballs, with a small wick pointing out of the top of them. When they were first made as **lethal weapons**, medieval French soldiers were reminded of another familiar object, and so they named the grenade after it. Can you guess what it was they were thinking of?

A. **A ball of string**

B. **A balloon**

C. **The pomegranate fruit**

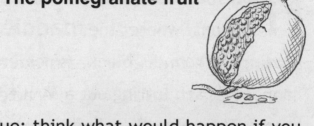

(Clue: think what would happen if you threw a grenade at someone!)

ANSWER. C!

'**Grenade**' is a shortened version of *pome granada*, the Spanish term for the pomegranate fruit — it means literally 'many-seeded fruit'. A 'grenadier', which today means a soldier in the first regiment of the royal household infantry, used to mean a pomegranate tree before it meant 'grenade-thrower'.

It might not have just been the roundness of the fruit that made those medieval fighters choose its name for their weapon. The result of an explosion from as grenade would be lots of blood and guts — a bit like a bright red, squashed fruit and its pips. Ugh!

What a thrill!

If we say '**we're thrilled**' about something, we're really happy about it. Now imagine you are a jouster in a medieval tournament, mounted on your horse, helmet down and ready to do battle. Your contest will thrill the crowd gathered to watch, but it might also thrill someone or something else, too.

Have a guess who or what...

A. **Your opponent in the jousting tournament. To 'thrill' once meant to 'stab' or 'pierce a hole' in something.**

B. **Your horse. To thrill someone was to hold them completely in your power.**

C. **Your nose, which would be pierced with a stud displaying the coat of arms of your master.**

ANSWER: A!

The earliest meaning of '**thrill**' was to pierce a hole in someone or something. The sort of hole a pointed weapon like a jouster's lance could make.

So you would certainly NOT be thrilled to be thrilled, if you see what I mean.

By the way, those nose studs in answer C were a bit of a trick. Nose piercings weren't really in fashion then, but noses are connected to 'thrills' in another way, for the word 'nostril' was once a 'nose-thrill' — in other words, a nose-hole.

Simple!

Boom!!!

Some words are created to sound like the thing they describe — like 'fizzle', 'burp', 'hiccup', 'chatter', and 'squelch'. This kind of word-making is called '**onomatopoeia**'.

Nothing strange about that, you're thinking, and you're right. What might surprise you, though, is the meaning of one of those words when it was first used 500 years ago. The original meaning of '**fizzle**' was 'to break wind without noise' — in other words, to **fart silently**! If we say something 'fizzles out' today, we mean it loses its power and fades away. Just like a windipop that no one else notices.

Now, what's the opposite of a quiet, er, fizzle? It's one that *explodes* of course, and that has a very funny story behind it...

If you've ever been to a panto, you'll know that the baddie is always loudly **booed** and **hissed** at! In ancient times, *every* actor, even in serious plays, faced that horrible possibility. This time, though, it wasn't just booing and hissing, but some deafening clapping too.

Today, of course, we associate clapping with approval, but in the days of Roman theatre it could the opposite. And so if an actor wasn't particularly good, the audience would clap VERY loudly.

The Latin word for clap was *plaudere* — which is where we get the word '**applause**' from. *Explaudere* meant to clap someone OFF the stage — *ex* meant 'off' or 'out'. So when someone 'exploded' in the theatre, they weren't struck by a bomb or a stick of dynamite. They were simply forced to leave the stage!

Totally toxic!

Have you ever seen one of these signs, warning you that something is *deadly* poisonous and contains **TOXIC WASTE**?

The story of the word 'toxic' might make you shudder. The grinning skull might also give you a clue!

'Toxic' comes from a word used every day by the ancient Greeks — *toxon*.

Back then, a ***toxon*** was an arrow, shot from a bow and used as a lethal weapon against the enemy. And what made them even deadlier was the cunning trick of dipping them in bubbling poison. This powerful killer became so notorious that *toxon* began to take on the meaning of the poison itself rather than the arrow, which is how 'toxic' passed into English and why it means deadly poisonous today. '**Intoxicated**', meanwhile, which is usually applied these days to someone who has drunk too much alcohol, originally described someone who had been speared by those treacherous arrows.

So, next time you see a picture of **Robin Hood** shooting his famous arrow, or even the archers competing in the Olympics, you can tell everyone about their deadly ancestors!

Your money or ... Blast!

Hands up who likes algebra?

If you've screamed **NO!!!** at this page, I have a confession to make — algebra was my favourite bit of maths at school — I think it was because it felt a little like a secret code that I was deciphering. Well, love it or hate it — or perhaps you've not come across it yet — I bet you won't be able to guess how it all began...

The word *al* means 'the' in the language of Arabic, which is where the adventure of algebra first began. Alcohol and alchemy (the magic art of turning metals into gold) are also words that travelled all the way from the exotic East.

Back then, '**algebra**' didn't just mean funny mathematical symbols though — originally it was all about putting human bones back together! The Arabic *al-jabr* meant 'the reuniting', and *this* is exactly what surgeons and doctors used to do with broken bones: they would put them back together in the right place by 'setting' them. Perhaps the sight of a lot of complicated mathematical symbols reminded ancient mathematicians of a jumbled pile of bones — and that is why they called such formulae as 'x = y' 'algebra' too. Think of that in your next maths lesson, and try not to giggle (or groan)!

We've gone wrong somewhere ...

Who's for the chop?!

Imagine the blood-curdling screams of a victim on the guillotine, that tall frame with a razor-sharp blade that was once used to slice off the heads of prisoners condemned to death. The guillotine was used hundreds of times during the French Revolution, often in front of huge crowds, but can you believe it was actually invented to make the chopping off of heads LESS painful?! Before then, swords were used, and they didn't always work very well, causing a lot of, er, mess. Of course, this punishment was only for the nobles — the common people were usually hanged.

And this is where Joseph Ignace Guillotin came in. He was a French doctor who recommended the use of a 'kinder' and quicker beheading contraption for everyone. And he also gave his name to the grisly machine.

'Guillotine' is what is known as an 'eponym' — an object that is named after its inventor. There are lots of them in English, each with a hidden story behind them.

Jules Léotard, for example, was a

French trapeze artist who gave his name to the all-in-one suit still worn by gymnasts today.

The word '**panic**' comes from the Greek god Pan, whose sudden appearance from the woods once terrified people.

The '**biro**' was invented by Lazslo Biro, and the 'Bunsen burner' by Robert Wilhelm Bunsen, a German chemist.

The spinning 'Catherine Wheel' that most of us love on Fireworks Night is named after the Christian saint, Catherine, who was condemned to death by a Roman emperor and killed on a spiked wheel, a terrible instrument of torture.

And the Garibaldi biscuit (known to some as squashed flea biscuits because of their appearance!) were named in honour of Guiseppe Garibaldi, a Italian general.

What a thug!

None of us like **thugs** — rough bullies are just not very nice. But where did the word come from? Try to guess which of the following stories are true.

A. 'Thug' was chosen as a word for a nasty bully because of its sound – 'thug' is similar to 'thwack' and 'thump', and suggests the noise of someone being hit hard.

B. The very first 'Thugs' were violent robbers in India, who had a horrible habit of stopping travellers and killing them as a sacrifice to the gods. They were famous for their particular method of killing, which was either by strong poison, or by strangling.

C. 'Thug' is a shortened version of 'the mug', because 'mug' is a slang term for the face or head – just where thugs used to strike their unlucky victims.

THUG!

ANSWER: B!

The very first Thugs were professional **robbers** and **murderers** in India (their other name was *phansigar*, which is Hindi for 'strangler'). They killed their victims as a sacrifice to Kali, the goddess of destruction. Tales of their crimes spread far and wide, and terrified travellers. In the end, thanks to very tough punishments (some even had their heads chopped off), they were stamped out, but people were still talking about them for many years to come. The Daily News newspaper from 1897 even reported that, 'When the Prince of Wales was in India, a

Thug criminal showed him how victims were strangled'. From these **scary** beginnings, the word passed into English to describe any violent criminal.

By the way, have you heard of the Sphinx, the terrifying creature from Greek myth with the body of a lion and the head of a woman? It used to stop travellers and ask them a riddle; if they got the answer wrong, it killed them. One of its favourite methods of doing so was (guess what?) by **strangling**, and its name probably comes from a Greek word meaning 'the strangler'.

Answers A and C weren't quite right, although English is packed with words that sound like the thing they describe (like '**burp**' or '**hiccup**'!). And 'mug' really is a slang term for the face, which is where the insult 'ugly mug' comes from (though best not use that expression yourselves!).

The final word...

I hope you've enjoyed discovering some of the yucky, **weird** and **WONDERFUL** stories behind some of our most innocent-looking words! I thought it would be fun to finish off with a story featuring some of the words from this book — the catch is that I'm going to use their original meanings rather than the ones we know today! See if you can make sense of it — maybe you could even try writing one yourself.

And above all, always remember: words are NEVER quite what they seem...

Weird World, weird Words...

Jack just managed to avoid a lasagne that was being emptied from a window above him as he walked to school. His mind was full of the scary dreams he'd had the night before, when geeks had been doing grotty things in front of a huge crowd. Luckily, they'd been given the thumbs up and were exploded off the stage, but the very thought of it was enough to make Jack fizzle and squirt. Just like that mistletoe bird, he thought (or the partridge, he remembered with a snigger).

As he passed a fruit stall, Jack saw a thug wielding a sword with his sinister hand and thrilling a sack of potatoes — practising for his real victims, Jack thought with a shudder. He grabbed a grenade from the stall and threw it at the man before running off towards the local stew — he could always hide in there if he needed to, and it would his sense of humour some good.

When the thug had finally gone, Jack ran out past the local barber, spotting the blood on the floor — eurgh. Even the doctor next door was treating a patient with a frog in his throat. The butcher's wasn't much better: the

smell of puddings drifted through the door and made Jack's arms go quite horrible. It was a right shambles.

What a morning. At least, Jack reminded himself, he was free — not like boys. And, even if he did sometimes run into fans and ferocious treacles, things could be a lot worse. He smiled to himself, and decided to peer into the windows of the local gymnasium for a laugh: even berserk people looked a bit silly in there!

The end.